WHAT NOT TO SAY

OFFICE & WORKPLACE

A Compendium of the
Worst Possible Things
You Can Utter Aloud

KNOCK
KNOCK®

LOS ANGELES, CALIFORNIA

WHAT NOT TO SAY

CONTENTS

WHAT NOT TO SAY

CONTENTS

WHAT NOT TO SAY

CONTENTS

INTRODUCTION

> "The blunders of one man often serve
> to suggest right ideas to another man."

Founding father Thomas Paine knew exactly what he was talking about. Unless you've taken a vow of silence at an ashram or are pleading the Fifth in the courtroom, you're probably susceptible to putting your proverbial foot in your proverbial mouth. We've all had moments in which we've uttered thoughtless, ignorant, insensitive, tactless, entitled, or just plain bone-headed remarks.

While faux pas can be made at any time and in any place, the workspace and office provide some of the most minefield-laden situations we face in our lives. Not only does the quality of our daily life revolve around successfully completing these one-on-one interactions, our very livelihood depends on not lousing things up in our career—or even in a part-time job.

That's where this book comes to the rescue. It's a handy reference guide for what to avoid saying in situations ranging from watercooler chat to quitting a job to being at the office party to having a job interview; a cheat sheet of no-go remarks when talking to people like the boss's spouse, a coworker, HR, or the office hypochondriac.

For instance, when talking to an angry customer, "I'm not paid enough to care about this" is a recipe for disaster. It's also probably best to avoid anything like "Do you do random drug testing?" during your onboarding. And never tell your boss "That's not my job." Chances are you'll end up having to consult this book for what not to say when getting fired.

Verbal gaffes are just one component of this book. In addition to a list of specific phrases that you should avoid, there are helpful sidebars with tips, tricks, and cautionary tales. And featured throughout the book are ten things one should never, ever, verbalize in the workplace under any circumstances—a veritable Hall of Fame of what not to say.

While some people have the amazing capacity to utter completely dunderheaded remarks and never pay the price, most of us are not so lucky. As turn-of-the-century horticulturalist and noted conversationalist Lady Dorothy Nevill remarked, "The real art of conversation is not only to say the right thing at the right place but to leave unsaid the wrong thing at the tempting moment." Or, as this quote attributed to Abraham Lincoln says, "Better to remain silent and be thought a fool than to speak out and remove all doubt."

WHAT NOT TO SAY IN
THE WORKPLACE, EVER

I'm telling!

WHAT NOT TO SAY TO AN

ANGRY CUSTOMER

1 It's amazing how you can say so many words that mean absolutely nothing to me.

2 Hold on, I can't find my "I give a shit" mask.

3 They say the customer is always right, but you're only a customer if I help you.

4 I'm not paid enough to care about this.

5 Do you need a diaper change?

6 You're going to be even angrier when you see what I put in your drink.

7 I'm willing to get fired for kicking you in the neck.

8 My last job cleaning monkey poop at the zoo had a more civil clientele.

9 The person who's paid to care about your complaint is at lunch.

10 I'm sorry, I don't speak dipshit.

WHAT NOT TO SAY TO YOUR

ASSISTANT

1   I need you to mail me some cocaine at the conference.

2   Do you know how to get rid of a body?

3   You don't want to hear what happened to my last assistant.

4   Type up a memo about how I'm firing you.

5   You know there's no professional ladder here, right?

6   Please shut the door, I need to weep for a bit.

7   What's your position on money laundering?

8   When the SEC comes, tell them I'm in Cabo.

9   I don't even know what I'm supposed to be doing.

10   I haven't been this busy since prison.

A COKE AND A SMILE MIGHT BE BETTER

Pepsi came under fire in 2017 for releasing a commercial depicting a Black Lives Matter rally on the verge of a riot until sexy, Caucasian, independently wealthy reality personality Kendall Jenner appears and hands out cans of Pepsi, immediately quelling the tension. Unsurprisingly, the internet exploded with derision—an entitled, white, would-be fashion model is not the ideal choice for the fantasy savior of the struggles minorities face in America. While no one knows what went down in Pepsi's boardroom when they hatched this hair-brained plan, we can still learn from its tone-deaf ideas. Before offering your own opinion, think about the bigger picture and use a little empathy. And Pepsi may be searching for a new advertising team, if anyone's looking for a gig.

WHAT NOT TO SAY
WHEN RECEIVING YOUR

BONUS

1. So we had a bad year?

2. This isn't enough for me to keep your secrets.

3. Cha-ching!

4. You call this a bonus?

5. Hey, I worked harder than that.

6. I can finally pay off my bookie.

7. I'm rich, I'm rich!

8. Where is the rest?

9. So much for "trickle down."

10. I do have you fooled, don't I?

BORED

1 Who brought beer?

2 I'm killing it in this Solitaire tournament.

3 Has anyone seen my pet rat?

4 Can I use someone's HBO Go login?

5 I can't believe they pay me to sit here!

6 Pen-click contest in my cubicle!

7 Let's start an office "burn book."

8 I know it's July, but who's in for Christmas caroling?

9 I wish I had more work.

10 Spin the bottle, anyone?

1 That's not my job.

2 You think you need an assistant? *I* need an assistant!

3 Oh, I had it in my calendar for *next* week.

4 I was out so late last night, I had to sleep in.

5 It wasn't my fault!

6 That's above my pay grade.

7 I thought we canceled that project.

8 I forgot to back it up.

9 I really need a personal day.

10 Good, fast, cheap: pick two.

MOTOR CITY MADNESS

Now that the extracurricular space of social media has become the province of corporate advertising too, the lines between work and play are blurrier than ever. Scott Bartosiewicz, the social media strategist for the aptly named New Media Strategies, should have been more careful when he signed onto Twitter to complain about their client Chrysler's hometown. Thinking he was tweeting from his personal account, he accidentally tweeted from Chrysler's corporate one: "I find it ironic that Detroit is known as the #motorcity and yet no one here knows how to fucking drive." Chrysler did not renew its contract with New Media Strategies, and Bartosiewicz was fired. A good reminder to always keep work and play separate.

STAND UP FOR YOURSELF, OR NOT

You've undoubtedly seen those standing desks. You know, the ones that are supposed to help with office workers' circulation or to fight cancer or something. Well, it turns out those do almost no more good than just sitting at your desk. And both of those options are bad for you. Researchers at the University of Illinois at Chicago found that people who stood at a desk had a negligible elevation in their metabolism when compared to their sitting coworkers. But researchers also found that those who sat in a chair that allowed them to swing or move their feet saw a significantly elevated metabolism, a 17 percent rise over those who simply sat or stood. So enjoy your expensive standing desk, but you still may want to go for a few walks around the office. We do not, however, recommend doing wind sprints in the hall.

WHAT NOT TO SAY TO THE

BOSS'S CHILDREN

1 Do you get treated as badly as he treats us?

2 How's that trust fund growing?

3 What's it like to grow up without a parent?

4 Would you like to go out sometime?

5 Get a job.

6 Can you put in a good word for me?

7 So you're the reason I can't get a raise?

8 Funny, I never hear anything about you.

9 I'm the one that actually does all the work.

10 And to think they never wanted kids.

WHAT NOT TO SAY IN
THE WORKPLACE, EVER

I'm reheating fish in the microwave.

WHAT NOT TO SAY TO THE

BOSS'S SIDEPIECE

1. How long have you been on the payroll?

2. Do you get benefits too?

3. Do you prefer sidepiece or sidechick?

4. That necklace you're wearing was supposed to be my raise.

5. How much is my silence worth to you?

6. He's never leaving his wife for you.

7. Mind if I tag you in this photo?

8. Have you met their kids?

9. How's the sex?

10. Of course everyone knows.

WHAT NOT TO SAY TO THE

BOSS'S SPOUSE

1   It's so great that you're cool with the strip clubs.

2   You're much hotter in person.

3   Maybe we can double date sometime?

4   I think she'd be a nicer boss if she got laid more often.

5   So I hear things are pretty bad at home.

6   That diamond looks so real.

7   Don't you wish he had a less attractive administrative assistant?

8   I recognize you from your Facebook photos.

9   I didn't know he was married!

10   I see where your daughter gets her good looks from.

WHAT NOT TO SAY DURING A

BRAINSTORM

1. But does that really push the envelope?

2. I need to get super drunk first.

3. That's a terrible idea.

4. What would Steve Jobs do?

5. Frankly, I do my best thinking while on the toilet.

6. I only want out-of-the-box ideas.

7. We tried that already.

8. We should all try some ayahuasca right now!

9. My brain hurts.

10. BOOOORING.

WHAT NOT TO SAY ON YOUR

BUSINESS CARD

1. Professional Jam Taster
2. Really Likes Minecraft
3. Unemployable
4. Visit Me on Myspace
5. Only Arrested Twice
6. Skilled Basket Weaver
7. Able to Act Like a Cat
8. Advisor to President Trump
9. Solid C Student
10. Constantly Trying Not to Fart

SISTERS, SPEAK UP

Hey, ladies, have the feeling that you're not getting proper credit in the workplace? Well, you're right. And it's been scientifically proven. According to a study conducted by researchers at the University of Delaware, when men speak up about how to better their team, they're seen as potential leaders. When women do it, however, it's not seen the same way, and they don't get considered for promotions or raises as often. Of course, women have known this since they first suggested their pack of cave dwellers try putting wheels on their carts and Orgnel of the Mountaintop took credit for the idea. The study offers no suggestions on how to remedy this, but let's just start with telling male CEOs to stop being such jerks, so that women no longer have to worry so much about what not to say.

WHAT NOT TO SAY TO THE OFFICE

CLEANING CREW

<u>1</u> Sorry about the mess in the trash can. I'm pretty hungover.

<u>2</u> Don't enter my office if there's a sock on the doorknob.

<u>3</u> Guess when you clean the bathrooms you can tell when it's been taco Tuesday, huh?

<u>4</u> Whatever you do, don't open that drawer.

<u>5</u> Where in the hell did you move my sticky notes?

<u>6</u> I need to work late. Can you come back at midnight?

<u>7</u> Please don't touch the crystals on my desk. They'll pick up your sad vibes.

<u>8</u> Uh, did you find my résumé in the copy machine?

<u>9</u> We'll provide hazmat suits upon request.

<u>10</u> I'm very easygoing—as long as you do everything exactly the way I want.

CLIENT

<u>1</u> You're so important to us that we take you for granted!

<u>2</u> Nag, nag, nag…

<u>3</u> You're not the boss of me, technically.

<u>4</u> We've found your appreciation of our skills is directly related to how much you pay us.

<u>5</u> I *am* paying attention!

<u>6</u> Someone woke up on the wrong side of the bed.

<u>7</u> Don't be such a baby.

<u>8</u> OMG—you're so gullible!

<u>9</u> It's been so long, I totally forgot you were here.

<u>10</u> We love our clients, and love means never having to say you're sorry.

<u>11</u> Do we *really* need to do these account reviews?

WHAT NOT TO SAY IN
THE WORKPLACE, EVER

If you're "nice" to me, I'll be "nice" to you.

COFFEE ORDER

1. Milk, sugar, the last shred of my dignity?

2. I guarantee nobody spit in this.

3. Studies show coffee causes cancer.

4. You sure you want this? You seem pretty jittery already.

5. Steve Jobs started out taking coffee orders too. And once he became rich and famous, he remembered all those people who had given him those coffee orders, hunted them down, and had them killed.

6. Throw a little extra change my way and I'll get you a cup of "coffee with benefits."

7. I don't take fussy coffee orders.

8. Coffee, nature's highly addictive amphetamine.

9. I tried them all—does this taste off to you too?

10. No way am I getting you pumpkin-spice anything.

WHAT NOT TO SAY AT A

CONVENTION

1. Who do I ask about getting hookers?

2. I was just told we'd all have to fight to the death.

3. Want to play hide-and-seek?

4. I'm not reading your name tag, I'm just staring at your boobs.

5. Your speech was great if you were aiming for totally boring.

6. I'm bad with names because I really don't care.

7. Party in my room later. I'll bring the gherkins.

8. I'm just here to have an affair.

9. I wonder if terrorists have events like this.

10. I really hate people.

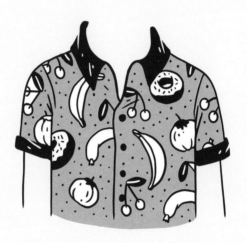

WHAT NOT TO SAY TO YOUR

COWORKER

1 If this cubicle is rockin', don't come a knockin'.

2 Whoops—sorry, I thought you were an intern.

3 Well, if you get fired, at least you can get unemployment.

4 This isn't personal—it's business.

5 This is just my day job.

6 I'm sure the boss will see how hard you tried.

7 Your concept of "work attire" is very interesting.

8 You explained it almost as well as I would have.

9 You might want to wait a while before you use the bathroom.

10 The only thing louder than your sneeze is your laugh.

DEADLINE

1 Didn't we postpone that project?

2 I need an assistant to help me keep track of things like this.

3 Nothing short of perfect will do for you.

4 I left it at my friend's house and she's out of town for a month.

5 I have it in my calendar for next week.

6 Everybody else failed to get me what I needed in time.

7 I tried so hard, but no matter what I did, I couldn't finish the project and take my government-mandated ten-minute breaks.

8 You didn't authorize overtime.

9 Do you want it fast, or do you want it right?

10 Every time I thought about the project, it stressed me out.

PHUB YOU

"Phubbing," the act of paying attention to one's smartphone rather than the person right in front of you, is not just for marriages anymore. Workplace leaders are doing it more and more, and they're unknowingly chipping away at team morale and productivity. What's more, Baylor University professors James Roberts and Meredith David, the authors of a study on this topic, found that bosses who constantly check their smartphones during meetings or conversations give employees a feeling of mistrust, which then negatively affects the way they see their own role or responsibilities. So, if you're a boss, put down the phone. And if you're an employee, try making emoji faces to keep their attention.

DON'T DRINK THE WATER

If you need an extra cup of coffee or tea to get through the workday, consider drinking from the toilet instead. It has fewer germs than the communal office coffee pot or teabags, according to research conducted by Initial Washroom Hygiene, a UK organization with a name so literal there's absolutely no question with what they concern themselves. Office teabags alone have, on average, seventeen times more germs than a regular ol' toilet seat. Researcher Dr. Peter Barratt says the culprits are employees who don't wash hands before making coffee or tea. The good news is the solution is rather simple: Keep any communal kitchen areas clean, and wash hands *before* making any food or drinks. Or perhaps see if you can find a hazmat suit in a sensible houndstooth pattern.

EGOMANIAC

1. I'm lucky to work with someone as self-important as you.

2. You're so humble—it's almost like you never won those awards you just told me about.

3. How do you fit all that ego into a normal-sized body?

4. It must be lonely at the top.

5. No one calls you bossy—just assertive.

6. I wish I were as comfortable in my skin as you are— you seem *very* comfortable.

7. I will always cherish the initial misconceptions I had about you.

8. Did your parents tell you often that you were special?

9. At least you're not phony. You don't mind being disliked for who you really are.

10. Making other people feel stupid doesn't make you look smarter.

WHAT NOT TO SAY WHEN GETTING

FIRED

<u>1</u> The truth is I quit doing this job six months ago. I've just been showing up to collect a check and the bennies.

<u>2</u> I never meant to stay this long in the first place.

<u>3</u> I'm the corporate leak.

<u>4</u> Thanks to you, my self-esteem has never been lower.

<u>5</u> Here's my resignation. Now you can't fire me.

<u>6</u> I'm too old for this crap.

<u>7</u> This job isn't exactly the gold mine you promised.

<u>8</u> Good—I don't want to go down with this ship.

<u>9</u> Poverty will be easier than working for you.

<u>10</u> If you give me a year's severance pay, I promise not to testify against you.

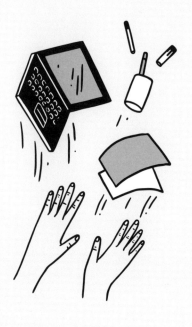

WHAT NOT TO SAY IN
THE WORKPLACE, EVER

I know you are, but what am I?

FIRING SOMEONE

<u>1</u> Here's your paycheck. You may notice it's pink.

<u>2</u> Good news! You get to file for unemployment!

<u>3</u> This is a box for your personal belongings.

<u>4</u> These are the days I hate being a boss.

<u>5</u> You can drink all day now if you want.

<u>6</u> First of all, I'd like to offer you the opportunity
to resign.

<u>7</u> I'd like to go over your severance package.

<u>8</u> We'll both be happier when you're free to pursue your
other interests.

<u>9</u> IT will help you transfer all your company files to the
server before you leave today.

<u>10</u> This may be your last chance to take advantage of the
employee discount.

<u>11</u> It's our fault. We never should've hired you.

<u>12</u> We're moving in a you-free direction.

<u>13</u> These security guards are going to escort you out of the building.

<u>14</u> We've found a machine that can do your job better.

<u>15</u> I share your pain, though I've never been fired.

<u>16</u> I'm sorry you won't be at the company holiday party this year.

<u>17</u> Hi! I'm your replacement.

<u>18</u> We're delighted to be able to offer you this career-change opportunity.

<u>19</u> There's no room for you on our new organizational chart.

<u>20</u> Welcome to Outplacement Training.

1 How lucky for you that nerds are so cool right now.

2 I'm impressed by your artificial intelligence.

3 You have more talent in your thumb than you do in the rest of your body.

4 I bet one day hot girls will be sorry they snubbed you.

5 You have so many online friends—maybe you could get some IRL.

6 It must be disappointing for people to meet you after seeing your avatar.

7 You're so commanding when you're trolling.

8 I'll bet you have a great virtual personality.

9 Hey, can you fix my computer?

10 With global access to the internet, intelligence is less and less important.

GOSSIP

1 Wind you up and you run someone down.

2 You never repeat gossip—you're the one who starts it.

3 You have a way of saying nothing that leaves nothing unsaid.

4 You say you're "speechless," then can't shut up.

5 Does the boss know you talk about her like this?

6 I've heard you detest gossip—when it's about you.

7 You call it "sharing opinions about other's life choices." I call it trashtalking.

8 I don't care that you're talking behind my back. I care that you don't have the facts straight.

9 Do you feel like tearing people down builds you up?

10 At least you never lie. The truth does much more damage.

WHAT NOT TO SAY WHILE

HIRING SOMEONE

1. This is an old-fashioned workplace, meaning we will sexually harass you.

2. We'll need to get you fitted for clown shoes.

3. What would you say is your biggest weakness when break dancing?

4. Don't mind all of the spiders.

5. I think you'd make a good July in our office beefcake calendar.

6. You're expected to grovel for your promotion.

7. I hope you like low pay.

8. You'll be a great fit until we fire everyone next week.

9. How do you feel about forced labor?

10. It's like working in a dungeon, but a really nice dungeo

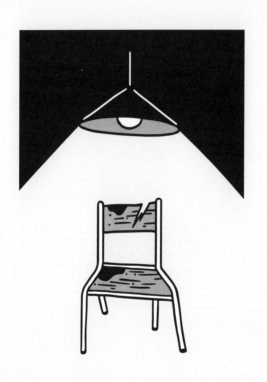

WHAT NOT TO SAY WHEN PLAYING

HOOKY

1. The cable's out, and I have to wait all day for the technician to arrive.

2. It's most contagious in the early stages, and I don't want to expose everyone at the office.

3. My husband's eighty-four-year-old great-aunt died suddenly.

4. I can't find my car.

5. I feel a migraine coming on.

6. I couldn't find a cheap babysitter.

7. I'm dedicating the rest of the day to self-care.

8. Two words: bad clams.

9. The vet said I had to watch Mr. Piddles all day to make sure he doesn't have a bad reaction to the medication.

10. My briefcase was filled with work I took home, and when I bent down to pick it up, I threw my back out.

HR

1. How many butts can I grab?

2. At lunch, the bartender suggested I expense the tab.

3. To build team morale, I think we should do a Cultural Appropriation Day.

4. I'm transitioning from male to ocelot.

5. We must stop the scourge of staffers who double dip in the guacamole.

6. Am I required to wear pants?

7. I hope you don't frown on taking office supplies home.

8. What's the company policy on gifting underwear?

9. It's only an illegal backroom poker game if you report i

10. I'd like for people to call me Boner McPeen.

WASTED TIME

Admitting you're coming in to work hungover is one thing, but getting whacked out on oxycodone while on the clock is quite another. Yet it's happening more and more according to a national poll by detox.com. Their results show that a staggering 70 percent of people have done drugs at work. And this isn't like smoking a joint in the alley before your shift at a comic shop. Thanks to the rise of opioid abuse coupled with a desire to perform well at work, we're talking everything from heroin to Adderall, and in industries like food service, health care, and education. It makes the days of hiding a bottle of Old Crow in your desk drawer seem positively quaint.

WHAT NOT TO SAY IN
THE WORKPLACE, EVER

We've always done it this way.

WHAT NOT TO SAY WHEN YOU'RE

HUNGOVER

<u>1</u> A couple of Bloody Marys and I'll be fine.

<u>2</u> Stop talking!

<u>3</u> You should be thankful I'm sober.

<u>4</u> I drink because I hate my job.

<u>5</u> Why does my tongue feel this way?

<u>6</u> And I'm still better at my job than you are.

<u>7</u> I'll just nap over here.

<u>8</u> I was even worse yesterday.

<u>9</u> I can't remember anything since Friday.

<u>10</u> No one mention vomit.

<u>1</u> There's gotta be mold in all these old buildings.

<u>2</u> Thousands of people touch those elevator buttons every day.

<u>3</u> Keyboards are the filthiest things in any office.

<u>4</u> I read that flu shots actually make you sick.

<u>5</u> When was the last time this conference table was cleaned?

<u>6</u> Looks like Marsha has pink eye.

<u>7</u> I found out toxic, non-organic cleaning supplies are used to clean the desks.

<u>8</u> Forgetting a meeting doesn't mean you have dementia.

<u>9</u> You should probably Google those symptoms.

<u>10</u> You know, I'm really not feeling so well.

WHAT NOT TO SAY IN AN

INSTANT MESSAGE

1. I hear we've got massive layoffs coming.

2. I've been having strong feelings about you and need to come clean.

3. Can you smell this in your office?

4. Do NOT eat the brownies in the break room.

5. I love how my desk hides the fact I'm not wearing pants.

6. Seen any good porn lately?

7. The guy standing at my cubicle talking to me… what's his name?

8. When you have a sec, can you come take a look at this growth?

9. God, I hate this job.

10. www.onlinegambling.com

<u>1</u> It's not so much a résumé as it is a tone poem.

<u>2</u> Didn't I go out with your daughter?

<u>3</u> I heard you'd hire any idiot.

<u>4</u> What's your policy on employees hooking up?

<u>5</u> My old coworkers were all morons.

<u>6</u> That's a dumb question.

<u>7</u> Nobody really *needs* a college degree.

<u>8</u> I know I'm good-looking, but I'm smart too.

<u>9</u> My psychic said I should apply for this job.

<u>10</u> Are you kidding about this salary?

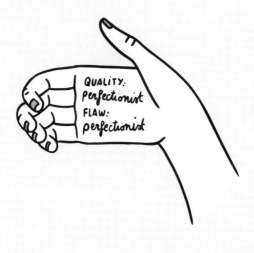

WHAT NOT TO SAY TO THE

IT GUY

1. You're so BASIC.

2. You're the portal to my cable.

3. How's that basement office treating you?

4. This shouldn't take too long, right?

5. Queue, cache, click…I told you I don't speak French.

6. Grab my dongle, would you?

7. Must be nice to just sit in front of a screen all day.

8. OMG, this whole time I thought you were a chatbot!

9. *Revenge of the Nerds* must be your favorite movie.

10. I love geeks!

DOWN FOR
THE COUNT

If you're one of the nearly 80 percent of people nationwide who experience downtime at work, you're costing your company a lot of money… Well, not you specifically, but you're part of the problem. Thankfully, the problem is not your fault. A study from the McCombs School of Business at the University of Texas at Austin shows that the blame most likely falls on your boss for scheduling your workload improperly or factors out of your control, such as waiting for a return call or assisting customers. If you experience such downtime, try constructing an elaborate pencil-launching device using only office supplies. It won't help anything, but it'll keep you busy.

JERK

---

1. My ideas sound so much better when you take them.

2. I wish I could be as ambitious as you, but I don't like the squishy sound it makes when I step on people.

3. Do you work hard to be a jerk, or does it come naturally?

4. You seem to have a black belt in brownnosing.

5. It's not everyone who can find the bad in every situation.

6. You must have been the coolest bully in high school.

7. Your passive-aggression really keeps me on my best behavior.

8. I don't think you're an asshole, but I seem to be in the minority.

9. You must have great upper body strength from climbing over all those people on the way to the top.

10. Your laugh is infectious, like syphilis.

WHAT NOT TO SAY IN
THE WORKPLACE, EVER

You can't
fire me—
I quit.

WHAT NOT TO SAY IN THE COMPANY

KITCHEN

1. Oh, that's my curry in the microwave. It'll just be another five minutes.

2. Freshen up my coffee, wouldya?

3. In the future, label your lunch so I know whose office I should return the empty Tupperware to.

4. I don't know about you, but these compliance posters are turning me on.

5. I'm fermenting my own kimchi in the office fridge.

6. The break room is a safe space, unless *Game of Thrones* was on last night.

7. For the office potluck I wore my edible underwear.

8. Is that a sausage in your pocket or is it just payday?

9. We could barely fit all these candles on your cake.

10. Who's gonna change this watercooler jug?

LATE TO WORK

<u>1</u> I'm okay now, but I actually threw up on the way over here.

<u>2</u> You should have seen the line at Starbucks, and you don't want me here without caffeine!

<u>3</u> The toilet overflowed and I had to wait for the plumber.

<u>4</u> My cat got out and I had the hardest time finding her.

<u>5</u> For some reason, my alarm didn't go off this morning!

<u>6</u> I had another panic attack.

<u>7</u> Traffic was a nightmare.

<u>8</u> I had to wait until my laxative kicked in.

<u>9</u> I was dealing with a personal matter.

<u>10</u> It takes hours to look this good!

WHAT NOT TO SAY ON YOUR

LINKEDIN PROFILE

1 I spent the majority of 2016 drunk.

2 Special Skill: Nude Trampolining

3 I once ate a pound of butter on a bet.

4 There's a gap in my employment history because I joined a cult.

5 My salary range is "bag of shiny rocks" to "used accordion."

6 Can cry on command.

7 My coworkers nicknamed me "Ugh, Him Again."

8 Reely gud spellr.

9 My idols include Mussolini and the cast of *Jersey Shore*.

10 Summary: I hate work.

1   Nobody likes me.

2   I'm going to sue.

3   How much cash do you have to keep me quiet?

4   It's like *Lord of the Flies* in here.

5   You can't handle the truth.

6   Working here was already bad enough.

7   They're all jealous of me.

8   You wouldn't want the holiday party photos to get out, would you?

9   It's all because of your toxic management style.

10   This place put the "ass" in harassment.

DON'T BRING YOUR FAMILY TO WORK

A large family dinner is actually the perfect place to compile a list of topics to avoid at the office: the news story your dad just read, Auntie Mabel's bankruptcy, Grandpa Gerald's hemorrhoids, that chick your brother banged, or all the amazing work Cousin Ingrid's church does brainwashing citizens of third-world countries. While families often strive to bait each other with controversial topics, your time at the workplace should be calm and focused on the task at hand. Not that you can't enjoy yourself, but unlike those pesky relatives, you probably want to play it safe and steer clear of politics, religion, sex, finances, or medical problems. And while you're at it, how terrible your boss is would also be a poor choice.

1 No cookies?

2 That's stupid.

3 Why are we here?

4 Game over? Crap!

5 You stole my idea!

6 Jawohl, mein fuhrer!

7 Who farted?

8 I'm so bored.

9 I'm sure that sounded like a good idea in your head.

10 [ZZZZZZ]

1 They sell deodorant practically everywhere now.

2 There seems to be something…growing…under
   your desk.

3 That candy bar dates from the first Bush administration.

4 Nice old coffe-cup collection.

5 FYI, the office dress code does not include black socks
   with sandals.

6 Who's eating the limburger sandwich?

7 Cologne is no substitute for bathing.

8 Your desk is now considered a biohazard.

9 My pen is out of oink—er, ink.

10 So clever of you to leave a crumb trail to your desk.

WHAT NOT TO SAY IN
THE WORKPLACE, EVER

Nyah,
nyah,
nyah.

<u>1</u> Could you turn the heat down a tad?

<u>2</u> Some idiot made decaf.

<u>3</u> One second I was smelling my pen, and the next secon you were waking me up!

<u>4</u> My chiropractor told me to rest my neck periodically ir order to avoid having to make a worker's comp claim.

<u>5</u> Too many carbs at lunch.

<u>6</u> Lucid dreaming is part of my brainstorming technique

<u>7</u> I was at the blood bank this morning.

<u>8</u> By accident I took the nighttime medicine.

<u>9</u> My keyboard was making the strangest noise.

<u>10</u> My doctor has prescribed daily medication when I'm stressed.

NONE FOR
THE ROAD

Is a flimsy excuse better than the truth? Frank Sinatra found out when he agreed to play the role of Billy Bigelow in the film *Carousel* while simultaneously maintaining a marriage to Ava Gardner. Showing up on location in Maine, where they were preparing to shoot in two separate widescreen processes, Ol' Blue Eyes gave the odd excuse that he hadn't signed on for two pictures, and drove off in his limo. But according to *Carousel* star Shirley Jones, Gardner had told Sinatra that if he didn't join her immediately in Africa where she was filming at the time, she would have an affair with her co-star, Clark Gable. Sinatra was sued by Twentieth Century Fox, and had two more years of drunken codependency to look forward to with Gardner.

<u>1</u> Two words: tax shelter.

<u>2</u> Sexual harassment won't be a concern at our startup since women can't code anyway.

<u>3</u> I don't know the meaning of the word "bubble."

<u>4</u> The good news is we've already started incurring debt.

<u>5</u> No one else would take a meeting with us.

<u>6</u> This is a great opportunity, and if you don't get on board, my dad will have to.

<u>7</u> The beauty is, we're also literally a laundering business.

<u>8</u> The terms of your ownership stake allow you to pick out the rug in the lobby.

<u>9</u> We like to call ourselves *Little* Tobacco.

<u>10</u> You'll regret it if you don't get in on the ground floor of this multi-level-marketing scheme.

OLD

1 Is your memory in black and white?

2 I appreciate your historical perspective.

3 You must be very wise too.

4 You can call it an "electronic typing contraption" if you'd prefer.

5 FYI, the internet is not a series of tubes.

6 Luckily for you, we allow employees to take naps throughout the day.

7 I'm guessing you won't be using our corporate gym.

8 You've got gravitas written all over your face.

9 Whippersnapper…is that a new app?

10 You bring a nice "vintage authenticity" to the team.

BASEBALL'S BEASTLY BOSS

Marge Schott, CEO and president of the Cincinnati Reds from 1984 to 1999, had a good side. Fans liked her, and she supported many charities helping animals and children. But when she opened her mouth, there was no doubt she was one of the all-time worst bosses. Schott was known for her slurs against African Americans, Asians, gays, and Jews. She opined that Adolf Hitler "was good in the beginning, but went too far." When a heart attack killed an umpire in the middle of a game, she responded, "Snow this morning and now this. I don't believe it. I feel cheated." Baseball's executive council suspended Schott in 1993 for "the most base and demeaning type of racial and ethnic stereotyping" and fined her $25,000. Eventually, she was forced out altogether, much to everyone's relief.

ONBOARDING

1. Do you allow napping on the clock?

2. Hope I get paid soon—my recreational drug habit doesn't pay for itself.

3. I'll just be doing this until my band gets signed.

4. Do you do random drug testing?

5. How important is it for me to actually show up?

6. I have a huge problem with authority.

7. Do any staffers keep valuables in their desk drawers?

8. How strict is your sexual harassment policy?

9. Is there an office where I can spend the night?

10. Screw you.

OVERLOOKED FOR A PROMOTION

<u>1</u> Time to start stealing stuff.

<u>2</u> This is the thanks I get for putting in the minimum effort.

<u>3</u> If you need me, I'll be at my desk, job hunting.

<u>4</u> I kissed all that ass for nothing.

<u>5</u> That's OK, the embezzlement should cover me.

<u>6</u> Expect me in my pajamas from now on.

<u>7</u> Thankfully, I don't give a shit about this job.

<u>8</u> Looks like it's time for a health-code violation.

<u>9</u> Why do I even show up sober?

<u>10</u> I understand—the boss's coke habit won't pay for itself.

WHAT NOT TO COMPLIMENT

You can compliment women at your workplace without making them feel harassed. It's really not that difficult. Need a few guidelines? Don't compliment her body or her appearance—there's no place for this in a professional environment. Don't tell her she's great at something, for a woman. (Uh, that's not a compliment.) Avoid telling her something she has done is adorable or cute or use any words that could describe a baby hedgehog. Don't use a term of endearment— avoid anything from sweetheart to candylamb. Don't tell her she's prettier when she smiles. When it comes down to it, don't give a compliment to a woman that you wouldn't give to a man. Stay on the safe side—just compliment her actual work performance.

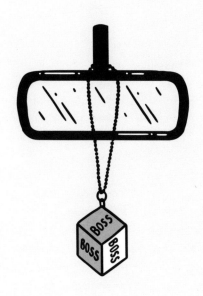

PARKING LOT

1 You don't get paid enough to drive a car like that.

2 I'll take you for a ride, baby.

3 What does your giant car compensate for?

4 Bob from accounting is hiding in your back seat.

5 Don't make me go back in there.

6 Who doesn't have free parking?

7 Where's my limo?

8 Only the little people pay for this.

9 Don't get your hopes up about the "employee of the month" parking spot.

10 Want to see me plug in my hybrid?

WHAT NOT TO SAY IN
THE WORKPLACE, EVER

Don't worry your pretty little head about it.

WHAT NOT TO SAY AT THE OFFICE

PARTY

<u>1</u> You give good email.

<u>2</u> This is just like the party they threw right before the last round of layoffs.

<u>3</u> I overheard the boss talking—what's a hostile takeover?

<u>4</u> I've been stealing office supplies.

<u>5</u> Remember the last holiday party? I don't.

<u>6</u> You should tell the boss what you really think of him.

<u>7</u> This is cool because I'm usually drunk at the office anyway.

<u>8</u> Oh, so *you're* the one who's not getting promoted.

<u>9</u> Does our health insurance cover medicinal marijuana?

<u>10</u> Underneath my clothes, I'm wearing nothing but sticky notes.

<u>1</u> This is going to hurt.

<u>2</u> Wait—do you work here?

<u>3</u> Before we start, you might want to get some tissues.

<u>4</u> Obviously, you didn't know about the hidden cameras.

<u>5</u> Close the door so no one hears the screams.

<u>6</u> I love this feeling of power.

<u>7</u> Do you want a blindfold?

<u>8</u> I need to take my anger out on someone.

<u>9</u> You're a great employee, but no one will ever know that

<u>10</u> What's in this for me?

WHAT NOT TO SAY
WHEN ANNOUNCING YOU'RE

PREGNANT

1 Didn't you notice my boobs getting bigger?

2 Turkey baster!

3 We had to have SO MUCH sex.

4 When is my baby shower?

5 Thanks for showing me how not to parent.

6 Want to know what position worked best?

7 It was conceived on that conference table.

8 I was just working here for the health insurance.

9 I registered for onesies, blankets, a bouncy seat, and a new job.

10 I need to start my leave before the mucous plug drops.

Lots of people fantasize about quitting their job in a spectacular fashion. Flight attendant Steven Slater discovered that this isn't really a great strategy. In 2010, Slater famously quit his job at JetBlue. He was particularly stressed at the end of a flight, so grabbing the PA mic, he announced (with several choice profanities) that he was quitting. He then nabbed a couple of beers from the cart, activated the emergency chute, and slid to the tarmac. Thanks to the internet, he quickly became a national hero. However, the ending wasn't so hilarious. Slater was charged with several felonies and was sentenced to one year probation, mandatory mental health counseling, and drug and alcohol treatment. He also had to pay Jet Blue $10,000 for the chute. Perhaps an email would have been better.

QUITS

1. Enjoy moving on to greener cubicles.

2. Now we don't have to tell you how much we hate you.

3. Who'll force me to listen to stories about her cats?

4. I'll miss all the time I didn't get to know you.

5. Are you sure this is a good move considering you have no work skills?

6. I'll need to spread rumors about someone else now.

7. Did you get another job or just give up on being employed?

8. I didn't even know you worked here.

9. Are you going to keep sleeping with the boss?

10. Good—we already Photoshopped you out of the company photos.

QUITTING

1   I refuse to continue covering for your incompetence.

2   I can't work for a boss who doesn't understand my genius.

3   I've learned so much from you that it's time to start my own business.

4   I had a vision—it's not this.

5   I'm going to miss our Saturday morning meetings and midnight conference calls.

6   I want to leave while I still have some dignity.

7   I got a concussion from the glass ceiling.

8   I look forward to training my replacement.

9   This isn't business, it's personal.

10   I haven't forgotten about company loyalty. I've just chosen to be loyal to another company.

<u>11</u> I appreciate your holding my job open for me and paying high-level temps during my six-month maternity leave, but now that the baby's here, my priorities have changed.

<u>12</u> I can no longer deny my dreams.

<u>13</u> I'm dropping out of the rat race.

<u>14</u> I've decided to go freelance.

<u>15</u> I've decided to become independently wealthy.

<u>16</u> I've just made my last pot of coffee.

<u>17</u> I'm really a creative!

<u>18</u> I was meant for bigger things.

<u>19</u> You can pick up your own damn dry cleaning.

<u>20</u> Although it's a thrill to see my ideas implemented, it's no longer fun watching you get all the credit.

WHAT NOT TO SAY
WHEN ASKING FOR A

RAISE

<u>1</u> Do you mind if I call my wife while we're doing this?

<u>2</u> The first offer sounds great.

<u>3</u> How much do *you* make?

<u>4</u> And this comes with a title change?

<u>5</u> You should be able to afford this since we've had all those layoffs.

<u>6</u> Now I can finally support my ex-wives.

<u>7</u> This is long overdue, am I right?

<u>8</u> This better be what I was asking for.

<u>9</u> After all, it's only money.

<u>10</u> I've also got some vacation time I'd like to put in.

Alexander Kuzmin, mayor of the Siberian town of Megion, banned city workers from using certain phrases, including "I don't know," "What can we do?" "I was on vacation," "There is no money," "It's not my job," "It's impossible," and "I'm having lunch." A framed list of all twenty-seven prohibited excuses hangs next to Kuzmin's office. Those who refuse to uphold the ban "will near the moment of their departure." In the United States, it seems like far too many bureaucrats think that they can get away with excuses like these, but it wouldn't be wise to tempt your boss to make an example of *you*.

WHAT NOT TO SAY IN
THE WORKPLACE, EVER

Shall we take this outside?

<u>1</u> His sex life makes yours look tame.

<u>2</u> Tell anyone else and I'll have to kill you.

<u>3</u> We're taking bets on how long before you're fired.

<u>4</u> I found out when I hacked his email.

<u>5</u> I hate to speak ill of anyone, but…

<u>6</u> People hate him more than they hate you.

<u>7</u> Juicy gossip is the only thing that makes this job bearable.

<u>8</u> I *knew* that was how she got the promotion.

<u>9</u> You'd better hope I never get any good dirt on you.

<u>10</u> You hear a lot when you hide in a bathroom stall.

WHAT NOT TO SAY AT A COMPANY

RETREAT

1. Who's hungover?

2. We're going streaking!

3. Hopefully I'll see you all here next year.

4. It's a cash bar, everyone.

5. Is the pool clothing-optional?

6. Will we have coed hotel rooms?

7. Can I bring my kids?

8. It felt consensual to me.

9. I'm here for the trust falls.

10. Clearly, I didn't bring enough underwear.

SLACKER

1 It's always a pleasure to cover your ass.

2 Some of us actually work for a living.

3 You really put the "ass" in "assistant."

4 It's nice to know that I can always count on you to flake.

5 This is so impressive…for you.

6 You spend more time on the couch than a therapist's dog.

7 How much are you getting paid?

8 You make sloths look ambitious.

9 I know you're trying—very trying.

10 It's not everyone who can be satisfied with mediocrity.

WHAT NOT TO SAY WHEN CAUGHT

STEALING SUPPLIES

<u>1</u> I was making you a surprise.

<u>2</u> I'm just alphabetizing everything.

<u>3</u> We're playing hide and seek. You're it!

<u>4</u> Maybe you should pay me more so I don't have to steal to get by.

<u>5</u> These aren't free for the taking?

<u>6</u> The front desk said I could.

<u>7</u> I'm just sniffing the highlighters.

<u>8</u> I'm part of a company-wide supply-closet-theft sting operation.

<u>9</u> I was just napping in here.

<u>10</u> I can make a fortune on the sticky-note black market.

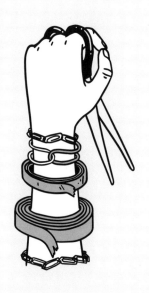

1. You said this was a good job.

2. I need another drink.

3. Damned meds aren't working.

4. I don't get paid enough for this.

5. [primal scream]

6. Anyone have an extra Xanax?

7. I knew I'd hate this job.

8. What's the office policy on drinking?

9. I quit! I quit! I quit!

10. Attica! Attica! Attica!

While it may be tempting to terminate an employee using remote or electronic means (look no further than President Donald Trump's reported firing of Rex Tillerson via Twitter), it may not be a good choice. In 2006, Radio Shack was vilified in the press for firing four hundred workers in an email. They dug the hole deeper by using unclear corporate speak: "The workforce reduction notification is currently in progress. Unfortunately, your position is one that has been eliminated." Wonder if the consultant who recommended that obtuse approach has had his position eliminated? One can only hope.

DON'T BE
A QUITTER

High on the list of what not to say are the words, "I QUIT!" While it's extremely gratifying to quit your job, it may be more financially beneficial to get yourself fired. Termination without cause can reap you unemployment, and if you play it right, severance pay. "Cause-free" is key, and clever self-sabotage is tricky, so be sure to tread carefully. Start by extending your lunch breaks and getting sick a lot. Then, if you have kids, use their assorted illnesses as an excuse for even more lost time. Escalate to (slightly) sloppy work, misunderstanding, general grumpiness, and moping around. No one is going to want you there!

WHAT NOT TO SAY AROUND THE

WATERCOOLER

1. I'd talk about what I watched on TV, but we all know TV is evil.

2. This is helping sober me up.

3. Let's discuss our STDs.

4. So, the boss is a real jerk, huh?

5. I heard the new guy is an elf.

6. Hang on, let me record this.

7. I thought this was an open-carry workplace.

8. I'm bringing a date to the office party instead of my husband.

9. What porn do you prefer on your work computer?

10. It's a shame that they've scheduled this building for demolition today.

WHAT NOT TO SAY IN
THE WORKPLACE, EVER

Just remember— my dad is the boss.

WHAT NOT TO SAY TO YOUR

WORK SPOUSE

1. Let's consummate this marriage!

2. I want a work divorce.

3. We should open up this relationship.

4. Honey, can you take out the trash?

5. I think we should start seeing other coworkers.

6. Let's get monogrammed office supplies.

7. How have you managed to stay married?

8. Wanna have a threesome with Judy in accounting?

9. I'm the closest thing to a real spouse you'll ever get.

10. When do I get my conjugal rights?

WHAT NOT TO SAY WHEN FILING FOR

WORKER'S COMP

1. I pulled a hammy bending over to kiss the boss's ass.

2. My eyes hurt from all the rolling.

3. Does a trampoline have to be on company property for this to apply?

4. I'm not physically hurt, but this job is crushing my soul.

5. I hit my head while pretending to blow my brains out.

6. Can I get compensation if I injure someone else?

7. I didn't think juggling knives in the break room would end this way.

8. How badly do I need to be injured to not come into work?

9. They should make computers softer so people don't get hurt when they punch them.

10. Can you just make the checks out to O'Hara's Pub?

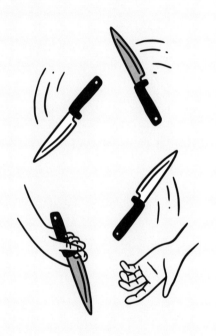

WHAT NOT TO SAY WHEN

WORKING FROM HOME

1. Just let me flush first.

2. Perhaps I should have told you my office is clothing optional.

3. Hang on—I need to apply more sunscreen.

4. My kid typically stops screaming after an hour or so.

5. "Face to face" and "collaboration" are totally overrated.

6. This desk chair should look familiar—I took it from the office.

7. My commute is killing me.

8. I don't know how you nine-to-fivers do it.

9. It's not sexual harassment if you do it to yourself.

10. Was I peeing too loud during that call?

WHAT NOT TO SAY BEFORE GOING ON

VACATION

1. Where I'm going, I'll need more than the usual shots.

2. I'll just use the goodwill I've built up so far and put it toward vacation time.

3. I'll be gone for two weeks: one week for vacation and one week to recover from the weeklong drug bender.

4. I'm not creating an out-of-office message since I never check my email anyway.

5. If my wife calls, tell her I'm "at a convention."

6. What's the charge code for a sabbatical?

7. When I'm gone, feel free to use the handicapped toilet.

8. Could you take care of my workload…and my dog?

9. I'm going to Amsterdam. Want some "souvenirs"?

10. Whatever you do, don't look in my drawers.

VACATION

1. I'd show you my tan lines, but I don't have any.

2. I picked up a side gig as a drug mule.

3. Guess my drinking will be on the clock again.

4. You'll see how my trip went when you watch the news coming out of Russia.

5. It's hard to care about all this after you've been to Topeka.

6. It turns out that when you're in another country, you can do all kinds of things that are illegal here.

7. I'm counting this as another vacation day.

8. If the Feds show up, you don't know me.

9. The trip made me realize what an asshole you are.

10. Wait until you guys get this virus I picked up.

WHAT NOT TO SAY TO ANY

UNDERLING

1. How about showing me your A-game?

2. Plenty of people would love to have your job.

3. If you can't stand the corporate heat, stay out of the corporate kitchen.

4. Let me ask you a question—do *you* think this is any good?

5. Maybe you just don't want it enough.

6. Have you ever thought about a different career?

7. This is really my fault—I knew you weren't right for this job.

8. I'd invite you to the meeting, but this is an *important* client.

9. You've got a very bright future ahead of you, somewhere.

10. Is this your best work?

REMEMBER NOT TO FORGET

It goes without saying (but we're still saying it here), lying is not a good strategy at work—or anywhere, really. However, if it is totally necessary, as with any excuse or lie, memory becomes critical. Whether your lie is challenged at a later date or you're called on to lie in order to cover up a previous lie (a slippery slope phenomenon known as the "ripple effect"), nothing exposes the liar like incongruous stories. If your lie involves others, make sure you synch up—but don't match, as one of the hallmarks of group lies is verbatim recitation. For frequent fibbers who want to avoid detection, consider keeping a lie journal.

YOUNG

1 I'd ask you to work late, but I think it's past your bedtime.

2 You don't know what we did before the internet, do you?

3 You think you can have it all—ha!

4 Life is short, and so is your list of accomplishments.

5 You remind me of when I was young and clueless.

6 Your youthful idealism makes me want to puke.

7 You think the world owes you, right?

8 Nobody but your parents think you're that special.

9 Your lack of experience is matched only by your surplus of ego.

10 Grow up!

Created, published, and distributed by Knock Knock
6080 Center Drive
Los Angeles, CA 90045
knockknockstuff.com
Knock Knock is a registered trademark of Knock Knock LLC

Illustrations by Laurène Boglio

This book is meant solely for entertainment purposes. In no event will
Knock Knock be liable to any reader for any harm, injury, or dam-
ages, including direct, indirect, incidental, special, consequential, or
punitive arising out of or in connection with the use of the informa-
tion contained in this book. So there.

Where specific company, product, and brand names are cited, copyright and trademarks associated with these names are property of
their respective owners. Every reasonable attempt has been made to
identify owners of copyright. Errors or omissions will be corrected in
subsequent editions.

ISBN: 978-168349177-4
UPC: 825703-50303-6

10 9 8 7 6 5 4 3 2 1